I'm Feelin' Kinda Gassy

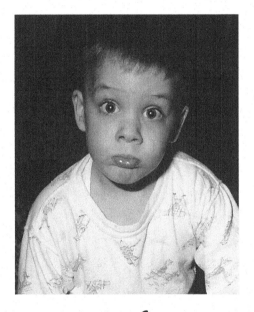

Fun poetic short stories

Gary L Tucker

Order this book online at www.trafford.com
or email orders@trafford.com

Most Trafford titles are also available at major online book retailers.

Printed in the United States of America.

ISBN: 978-1-4669-0318-0 (sc)
ISBN: 978-1-4669-0317-3 (e)

Trafford rev. 11/08/2011

www.trafford.com

North America & International
toll-free: 1 888 232 4444 (USA & Canada)
phone: 250 383 6864 ♦ fax: 812 355 4082

About the book

This book is filled with contemporary poems written as mini short stories with a message. A few are waiting for someone to attach a melody, perhaps you. The **fun** poems will make you laugh and the timid are sure to blush. The **inspirational** poems will cause you to think about your eternity and the freedoms Americans share. My poems of **love** include humor with a twist and you may learn something from poems for **life's lessons**.

You can find a smaller version of my poems in **Oh Lord, Tell Me Why,** which includes all my inspirational poems plus a few others that are suitable for church.

I wish to extend special thanks to the Pearce brothers as they traveled the world as soldiers in the United States Army. To all who choose a life of servitude I offer a heart felt thank you.

Thank you, Gary Tucker

Edited and photo arrangements by Gary Tucker.

Contents

Fun Poems

Inspirational Poems

Poems of Love

Poems For Life's Lessons

Fun Poems

I'm Feelin' Kinda Gassy

Written by Gary Tucker 9-2-2010 ©

Pass me the Gas-Free 'cause I'm feelin' kinda gassy
It may not be classy when I'm feelin' quite so raspy
Don't think I'm being passé when I say we all get gassy
So pass me the Gas-Free 'cause I'm feelin' kinda gassy.

Took the wife and kids to an all you can eat buffet
They had every kind of food there even fish called orange ruffet
But, when I saw those spare ribs I just couldn't get enough
I went back for more and more and I ain't talkin' guff.

While driving home that night I knew somethin' just weren't right
We're all in for a long ride, a long ride home tonight
My innards were unnerving feeling all those wiggles
Then I started burping and felt some bubbly jiggles.

Something inside me was trying to get out
"Oh! Oh! Oh!" I cried out with a shout
Felt like one of those aliens I saw in a sci-fi movie
"Oh! Oh! Oh!" Except this really wasn't groovy.

I could feel the pressure building but there was just no shielding
There were small explosions; hope nobody heard them
Followed by aroma; I tried to hold it in
I tried to hold it in but here we go again.

Pass me the Gas-Free 'cause I'm feelin' kinda gassy
It may not be classy when I'm feelin' quite so raspy
Don't think I'm being passé when I say we all get gassy
So pass me the Gas-Free 'cause I'm feelin' kinda gassy.

Do yourself a favor this ain't somethin' to be savored
Pass me the Gas-Free and roll your windows down. ©

Pucker Up, Boy

Pucker up boy, 'cause we're gonna kiss
Don't play coy do it like this
Let our lips come together in sweet wonderful bliss
Pucker up boy, get ready for my kiss.

You're driving me wild in that skimpy t-shirt
Flexing your muscles while working in the dirt
One foot on the shovel, two hands on the pole
Bending and turning while digging a hole.

Scoop a load of dirt and toss it in the air
Over your shoulder, dust flying everywhere
Put the shovel in the ground without any strain
The way you twist and turn drives me insane.

As the day goes by I see you working on your tan
My, Oh, My, what a beautiful hunk of a man
Reveling chiseled abs like a stone statue
I can wait no longer let our kissing ensue.

Pucker up boy, 'cause we're gonna kiss
Don't play coy do it like this
Let our lips come together in sweet wonderful bliss
Pucker up boy, get ready for my kiss.

I've been watching you for some time
My pheromones tell me you're in your prime
You look so good even covered in grime
Before the quittin' bell chimes you're gonna be mine.

With sweat on your brow in the noontime sun
You're lookin' so hot in more ways then one
When your digging is done what will you do?
Hear what I say if you haven't a clue.

Pucker up boy 'cause we're gonna kiss
Don't play coy do it like this
Let our lips come together in sweet wonderful bliss
Pucker up boy, get ready for my kiss.

Just close your eyes and you won't miss
Pucker up boy, it's you I'm gonna kiss
Just move your lips like a hungry fish
Pucker up boy, come get some of this. ©

Written by Gary Tucker
5-14-2011

Doctor Michelle

Doctor Michelle is a beautiful belle
A professional in dysfunctional health
Men come to this belle from miles around
Many fly in from far away towns.

With high heels and slender legs
A short dress attention begs
Long flowing hair, so lovely and fair
A sweet angelic face radiates with pure grace.

A soothing voice relieved my anxiety
I can tell this belle is high-class society
Gazed into hazel eyes soon to realize
Escorted to a room for an unforgettable surprise.

Doctor Michelle turned on some switches
Then proceeded to remove my britches
Soft music played as lights dimmed low
I was wondering where this might go.

Being examined with soft gentle hands
This doctor knows how to handle a man.
"We'll fix your dysfunction without any pills
I'll ready the suction so try to lay still."

Wasn't long before blood was flowing
I was ecstatic to feel something growing
Nearly forgot how to feel such pleasure
Wish my wife would examine my treasure.

She said, "I need to know if you're fully cured,"
What Michelle did next made my eyesight blurred
"Oh! Oh!, Doctor, now you know I'm healed
Wish you knew how wonderful it feels."

Looking at me with a great big smile
"I thought you knew what's behind this style
I know exactly how you feel 'cause it's a known fact
Professionally I'm Michelle but friends call me Jack." ©

Written by Gary Tucker
7-13-2011

Le Bare Derriere

I needed something to renew my health
So I took a vacation, just me and myself
Didn't care where, just had to get away
Found myself driving down Coastal Highway.

Came to a place called, "Le Bare Derriere"
Sounded romantic so I pulled in there
Parked my car and entered the lobby
Soon to be greeted by the host named Bobbie.

She was so lovely as she said with a smile,
"Take your clothes off and stay a while"
Being naïve not knowing what she meant
I continued checking in and paid for the rent.

Feeling a bit hungry I grabbed a bite to eat
Then proceeded to their private beach
A sign on the gate said, "No one under eighteen"
I was happy to see no kids would bother me.

Onward and forward without turning back
Until what I saw stopped me in my tracks
What my eyes were seeing I couldn't believe
I stood there frozen, unable to perceive.

I saw men and women completely bare
Playing in the sand tanning their derrieres
I never saw so much wagging and sagging
I never saw so many cracks and racks.

Out of the water came Bobbie the host
At least I think it's her without any clothes
Not kidding saying again with a smile,
"Take your clothes off and stay a while."

"I see you're new at this, but you'll be fine
Like many others I'll help you one step at a time,
Remove your sandals, feel the sand between your toes
Let's lose the shirt and we'll continue down below."

There was a long pause after my shorts hit the ground
Trying to build courage for one final round
Bobbie said, "If you need help with your last task
I'd be only to happy to help if you ask."

In a daze I must have said yes
Because the next thing I knew I was undressed
As I looked down I saw I wasn't wagging
So I ran for the water to conceal my flagging.

Bobbie followed me in and said with a grin
"It happens all the time with the working men"
Been a long time since it worked like it should
After all these years it feels really good.

From soothing water I'll depart eventually
But for now I'm enjoying this immensely
Ascending from the water onto the beach
Like Bo Derek, Bobbies' a ten and again I can be.

We walked along the seaside hand in hand
She helped me realize I'm still a workingman
Here I am bare showing off my lily-white derriere
Looking around I see nobody cares.

I think I found my new favorite resort
Didn't have to go far; don't need a passport
Discovered what I needed with out much wealth
I'm sure the doctor would be pleased with my health.

If you need something to renew your health
Take a vacation, just you and yourself
Don't care where; just have to get away?
Take a drive down Coastal Highway.

When you come to "Le Bare Derriere"
You've arrived and look for Bobbie in there
Be prepared for the time of your life
Just be sure you don't bring your wife. ©

Written by Gary Tucker 7-11-2011 ©

Ever wonder why so many men need medication?
Perhaps all they really need is spousal stimulation.

Saggin' Sally

My weight was more than I could tally
My mountains sank into the valley
Until I met Doctor O'Malley
They use to call me Saggin' Sally.

My derrière was more than I could bear
I have two feet somewhere down there
It's hard to believe I use to be thin
Don't remember when I saw only one chin.

Who knew a nip and a tuck and all the fat they sucked
Would bring me such good luck
For this new look I paid a lot of bucks
And worth every penny for this state of flux.

As time goes by I grin with a single chin
I see two lovely feet I can even reach
My mountains returned to their former glory
Appearing on TV with my transforming story.

Now with a smile after runnin' five miles
I don't have to sit and rest a while
As if in style time turned back its dial
I'm lookin' bodacious feelin' young and wild.

As I go about my day, torpedoes leading the way
I sing a happy song so gay
Thanks to Doctor O'Malley, I'm no longer Saggin' Sally
Men line up to dilly-dally.

I'll let you in on a secret, I'm sure you won't regret
Doctor O'Malley has the magic touch
With a nip and a tuck and all the fat they suck
Should bring you such good luck.

For this new look you'll pay a lot of bucks
And worth every penny for this state of flux
So get off the couch and climb into your truck
Drive on down to begin your new strut.
With a nip and a tuck and all the fat they suck
Should bring you such good luck.
Tally-ho, Sally, Tally-ho. ©

Written by Gary Tucker
5-23-2011

Man Trap

Written by Gary Tucker 5-17-2011 ©

You don't hold me close and tight
We don't romance in moonlight
There's no spark in your kiss
My advances you resist.

We don't love like before
Seems our love boat has run ashore
I'm not what your heart yearns for
You don't say you love me anymore.

You're too often late for our dates
The elusive big one makes me wait
You don't change for special occasions
Dressed to fish like on vacation.

They say, "If you can't beat them join them,"
So I've changed my coarse to win
With my new pole, my new goal
Is to hook a man at his fishin' hole.

Washed some new tank tops and put them in the dryer
Round and round they go getting smaller and tighter
Without a brazier I look like a new playmate rendition
Why I might even win a wet t-shirt competition.

Bought me some short shorts and made them even shorter
If they work, as planed I'll have to place another order
On this camping trip six-inch heels is what I need
When I'm stuck in the muck he'll have to rescue me.

I act helpless and coy not knowing what to do
Coming over to help me, it's he who has no clue
He shows me how to bait a hook and cast a fishin' line
"Oh, No!" I say, as I slip into the water right on time.

As he reels me in from the water wet clothes are un-concealing
I sigh a few faint quivers as curvaceous lines are quite revealing
His eyes bulging out and lower jaw open hangs
It worked! Hallelujah; Passion now flows through his veins.

As if he caught the big one he whisks me to a tent prepared
Satin sheets, air mattress, and scent of jasmine in the air
Shabby-Sheik for this outdoorsman; wet clothes fall to the floor
My man—trap's been sprung, I hooked what I been fishing for.

My pappy always told me good things are worth the wait
You can catch anything if you use the proper bait
I took his advice and bait my lure for the fisherman in my sight
One thing I'll never doubt, my pappy's always right. ©

Still in Seventh Grade

My dad was Mr. Universe
I really shouldn't boast
My mother Miss America
I got the best of both.

I'm six feet three
Have big feet, curly hair
Dark eyes
Muscles bulging everywhere.

I like it when the girls stare
I give a wink to show I care
Not just to ones most fair
A smile to all the girls I share.

The lady teachers find excuses
To keep me after school
They say I've got detention
For breaking all their rules.

Coach wants me on his team
Because I'm so strong and tall
"Show no Mercy" is his theme
The competition always falls.

In the locker room where
The boys see me bare
Beholding family jewels
"You rule!" They declare.

I'm eighteen years old
And still in seventh grade
I've broken many records
The honor roll I never made.

From school I'll not graduate
But, at least I'm having fun
I don't want those "A"s
By my rules "F" stands for fun, fun, fun. ©

Written by Gary Tucker
10-12-2010

Romantic Action

Men can't resist her magnetic attraction
She uses them for her satisfaction
Down yonder in Mississippi, Jackson
She's a lawyer looking for some romantic action.

For your broken sander she'll file a class action
When you've been slandered she'll get a retraction
If you've been hauled off to jail for of an infraction
She'll get you out in lieu of some romantic action.

You aught to see other lawyers' reaction
When they find her fees are but a fraction
She's on top of her game while others lose traction
She wins every time with some romantic action.

She hasn't missed yet with a jury of peers
In the minds of her colleagues she causes great fear
Her cleverness and beauty causes distraction
While her clients go free with no dissatisfaction.

When it's time for you to pay her bill
She'll be coming for you dressed to kill
Put away those checks made for cashin'
You better be ready for some romantic action.

Put away those checks made for cashin'
You better be ready for some romantic action. ©

Written by Gary Tucker
11-27-2010

Gus Maginnee

This is a story 'bout a man from West Virginee
A big mountaineer man called Gus Maginnee
He lived in a cabin high in the hills
Huntin' and trappin' and tendin' his stills.

Gus had a lovely daughter named Annabelle
She tended her chickens and had eggs to sell
A young man came by for eggs to buy
But, pretty Annabelle thought she'd be wise.

She said, "I sell eggs for the right price
All you have to do is treat me real nice
I'll make you an offer country boys can't resist
I'll give you one egg for a little kiss."

With a basket of eggs he finally went his way
He came back to buy more the very next day
Didn't take long for the men folk to discover
The new purchase price for eggs was uncovered.

Country boys lined up with jubilant anticipation
They couldn't resist Annabelle's gracious proposition
But, big Gus came home with his huntin' gun
My, oh my, you should a seen how fast they run.

It's a good thing Gus was out of ammunition
Or those boys would have felt his fiery intentions
Annabelle said to her pa in sweet angelic bliss
"How's a country girl spose to learn how to kiss?" ©

Written by Gary Tucker
5-19-2011 ©

Slasher, The Party Crasher

They call me the Slasher
I'm the party crasher
When I'm around you won't be bored
You never know what's in store
'cause I'm the Slasher
I leave my fans cryin' out for more.

Yeah! They call me the Slasher
I'm the party basher
I make everyone laugh so hard
They all think I'm the ace of cards
'cause I'm the Slasher
No one else comes close to par.

They call me the Slasher
I'm the party master
I leave 'em bustin' at the seems
My fans think of me in their dreams
'cause I'm the Slasher
They hold me in such high esteem.

They call me the Slasher
I'm the party smasher
All the ladies wish I was their hunky
We have more fun than a barrel of dunkeys
'cause I'm the Slasher
I can't hide that I'm funky.

If you're ever lookin' for some fun
Just call the Slasher I'm the one
My number's 555-SLASH-E-R
I'll come to you no matter where you are
We'll laugh all night 'till we see the sun
You'll be beggin' for more after the party's done.

To be perfectly honest though, some say I'm a hoax
They say I'm killin' them with my lousy jokes
It's because they're so lame I acquired this name
Said they'd shoot me if to their party I came
Now if you'll excuse me I must run
I see a posse comin' with their guns: why?

'cause I'm the Slasher
I'm the party master
But my jokes are disaster
That's why I'm a party crasher
I've been banned from their parties
And that's no laughing mater. ©

Written by Gary Tucker
10-12-2010

Doctor Written by Gary Tucker
11-28-2010 ©

Strip down and put on this gown
Leave your inhibitions at the door
There's no cause to be embarrassed
I've seen it all before.

I'll give you an exam
But, the gown must come off
It'll be over before you know it
Just turn your head and cough.

I'll help deliver your baby
So you can smother her with pride
I'm ready with my catchers' mitt
Push hard and spread 'em real wide.

I'll fix your broken bones
Reattach severed fingers
Put ice packs on your ankle
Prescribe something for smelly stinkers.

I'll reset your flattened nose
Mend your broken heart
But, first things first
Fill out this form so we can start.

I'll take pictures of your innards
Test your blood and give you shots
There's nothing you can hide
I'll tell you what you've got.

I'll stitch you when you're bleeding
Straighten out that kink
But, before you go
Leave a sample by the sink.

I'm a doctor and love what I do
Wouldn't change if I could
I repair broken bodies
I make people feel good. ©

Kicked in The Shin
and Socked in The Eye

Ate Granny's pie but said it wasn't I
For telling a big fat lie
Granny kicked me in the shin and socked me in the eye
Kicked me in the shin and s-s-s-socked me in the eye.

Passed a cop on his beat so I thought I'd be sly
I said, "Ahoy, Captain Bligh" as he came nigh
Bligh kicked me in the shin and socked me in the eye
Kicked me in the shin and s-s-s-socked me in the eye.

Went to the store but my pockets were dry
Merchandise from my hand proprietor tried to pry
The owner kicked me in the shin and socked me in the eye
Kicked me in the shin and s-s-s-socked me in the eye.

A boy fell off his bike and started to cry
I said, "You're not going to die; give another try"
The tyke kicked me in the shin and socked me in the eye
Kicked me in the shin and s-s-s-socked me in the eye.

Passed the vicar today but he walked on by
I shouted, "Friar! Get your head out of the sky"
Vicar kicked me in the shin and socked me in the eye
Kicked me in the shin and s-s-s-socked me in the eye.

Mother gave orders to clean my pig's sty
An irreverent sigh was the wrong reply
Mother kicked me in the shin and socked me in the eye
Kicked me in the shin and s-s-s-socked me in the eye. ©

Written by Gary Tucker 11-27-2010 ©

I Was Born a Cowboy

I'm a sharp shooter from a hundred paces
When playing poker I draw all the aces
I can rope a calf in four seconds flat
Nobody I know does it faster then that.

I fill my ten-gallon hat with dark wavy hair
My handlebar mustache causes quite a stare
I have spurs on my boots but I don't need them
Silver Dollar is my horse and she's my best friend.

I get up before dawn to work on the ranch
Overlooking the expanse I watch buffalo prance
Don't always make it home to sleep in a bed
Next to Silver and campfire I sleep instead.

I'm never alone with cowgirls by my side
They climb upon my saddle for a pony ride
The scent of manly rawhide is hard to resist
After all the galloping I treat them with a kiss.

I sit tall in my saddle driving my cattle
When I ride by snakes hold their rattle
I can ride the meanest bull at the rodeo
And be gentle as a dove doin' the do-si-do.

Ma taught me how to treat ladies good
And I always knew where my pa stood
I learned how to show courage with all my might
'cause sometimes you got to fight when it's right.

I was born a cowboy and I ride free
On the open range is where you'll find me
There's nowhere else I'd rather be
No troubles, no worries, no anxiety.

Ride along with me and you'll see
Where a boy becomes a man honestly
With hard work and dedication steadfastly
Like a cowboy you'll discover how to live free. ©

Written by Gary Tucker
6-14-2011

I'm Not As Young As I Use To Be

I'm not as young as I used to be
With out my glasses I can't see
My body aches all the time
I wasn't like this at age twenty-nine.

I'm a little sluggish, moving kind'a slow
My get up and go doesn't want to go
Those grandkids of mine run around so fast
With out a knap I wouldn't last.

For my birthday the wife gave me some pills
Said, "These will help us regain some lost thrills
You know I love you but you must agree
You're not as young as you use to be."

I went to the barber to get my hair cut
"Which one?" he laughed, clutching his gut
I have appointments and don't like to be late
But, this constipation is making me wait.

Went to the doctor 'cause I thought I was dying
How much time do I have and don't be lying?
He said, "Growing old isn't a crime
Take two aspirin, you'll be just fine."

The dentist is ready to pull my teeth
On with the mask, relax and breathe
He'll have new ones made for me
Because I'm not as young as I use to be. ©

Written by Gary Tucker
11-13-2010

26

Out of My Way

Woke up late cause I lost power
Without electric I took a cold shower
I have no dryer or curls for my hair
Wrinkled clothes are all I have to wear.

Hubby forgot to send his heavy load
Wouldn't you know the toilet overflowed
I'll have to do without morning coffee
Why does this have to happen to me?

Forgot to let Milo out the back door
Now there's a mess on the kitchen floor
It's to late to put on a face
I'll do it in the fast lane while driving with haste.

A driver cut me off in a little red pinto
So I made a jester and yelled out my car window
If you know what's good for you stay out of my way
Because this girl's having a really bad hair day.

Get out of my way so I can fly by
Hear the motor wine crankin' overdrive
Flashin' my lights and honkin' my horn
Get out of my way or regret when you were born.

Bogie pulled me over 'cause he saw me fly by
He clocked me goin' eighty in a fifty-five
Wished me good day as he gave me the ticket
Almost got hauled away when I told him where to stick it.

I'd call in sick if I could find my cell phone
Guess it'll have to wait till I get home
The calendar on the frig says I'm two weeks late
Sometimes it happens when passion won't wait.

Hubby came home from a long day at work
Could I be mistaken or is that lipstick on his shirt?
If you know what's good for you stay out of my way
Because this girl's having a really bad hair day.

Get out of my way so I can fly by
Hear the motor wine crankin' overdrive
Flashin' my lights and honkin' my horn
Get out of my way or regret when you were born.

One foot on the gas, one on the brake
Get out of my way you're making me late
If you know what's good for you stay out of my way
Because this girl's having a really bad hair day. ©

Written by Gary Tucker
8-1-2011

Yellow Camaro

Jumped in my car 'cause I have a need to go
I don't need a map; I just need to go
She's the most beautiful car on the road
Drivin' down the road in my yellow Camaro.

Droptop down, cruising eighty-five
Wind in my hair makes me feel alive
Weatherman says we'll have a sunny day
Got my sunshades on enjoying the rays.

My stereo's blarin' like a monsoon
I'm singin' along with my favorite tunes
Foot on the gas, no need to use the brake
Four hundred horses beg to accelerate.

Other cars move over so I can pass by
Hear the motor purr crankin' overdrive
This need for speed is so exhilarating
Faster and faster she's accelerating.

As the sun sets low I pull on the reigns
Horses slow down because they're well trained
The desert stars above sparkle and glow
Pulled off the road to enjoy their splendid show.

Fully reclined in my leather seats
My eyes got heavy and soon fell asleep
The morning sun's saying it's time to go
Headed down the road in my yellow Camaro.

Other drivers move over with envy in their eye
Hear the motor purr crankin' overdrive
This need for speed is so exhilarating
Faster and faster she's accelerating.

She's the most beautiful car on the road.
Drivin' down the road in my yellow Camaro.
Heads turn as she puts on a show.
Drivin' down the road in my yellow Camaro.
Feel tuned echoes from her magnaflows.
Drivin' down the road in my yellow Camaro.
Don't you know she was made to go?
Drivin' down the road in my yellow Camaro. ©

Written by Gary Tucker
8-5-2011

Inspirational
Poems

Oh Lord, Tell Me Why

Little girl don't you cry
Little boy dry your eyes
I know you're asking why
Oh Lord, tell me why.

The pain you try to hide
Reveals the hurt inside
When heartaches come in tides
You loose all sense of pride.

Don't be afraid if you can't walk
You need fingers to help you talk
When others point and gawk
Rise above them and don't sulk.

The disease that lives inside
An awful sickness there abides
Its growth does not subside
With medications you have tried.

If your eyes don't let you see
You get lost along your way
When the sun cannot be seen
I'll guide you to a brighter day.

When your mind is working slow
And it's hard for you to think
Take my hand and I will show
You how to bridge the link.

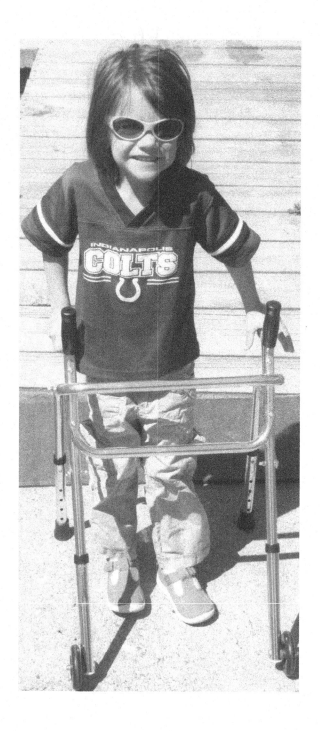

Little girl don't you cry
Little boy dry your eyes
I know you're asking why
Oh Lord, tell me why.

The imperfections we all share
Will some day fade away
New bodies with new clothes we'll wear
Come resurrection day.

No more loneliness or sorrow
Or cloudy days of rain
Look forward to tomorrow
We have so much to gain.

We'll no longer live in pain
No longer feel ashamed
We'll be smarter than any mortal
With new ingenious brains.

We'll play hide and seek
And throw a super fastball
Never tire; never sleep
Skip rope and that's not all.

We'll run and jump to the sky
We'll even learn how to fly
Our new bodies never die
We'll stop asking why.

We'll have new tongues for voicing
No need to speak with hands
With new ears will hear rejoicing
Throughout all the land.

If you wish to find relief
From your suffering and grief
A glorious day awaits you
If in Jesus you believe.

Special ones with special needs
Deserve a special love
When a hand is reaching out in need
Remember, God's watching from above. ©

Written by Gary Tucker
3-4-2011

As I was walking along in the mall a hand reached out to me. Looking at the face of this man I could tell he had special needs. I was honored to shake his hand. This ode is in honor of him. For those who believe, there really is some truth in the story of Superman.

Second Chances

He failed over and over again
No one gave him second chances
Before judging others
Consider your own circumstances.

If you think you're perfect
You're not alone
There's a long line of critics
Waiting to cast the first stone.

It's hard to say, "I'm sorry"
It's harder to say, "I forgive you"
You've been given second chances
Forgive the past and start anew.

When I was passed out in gutters
God gave me second chances
He left His ninety-nine to find me
Where no one dared to glance.

I was not in full agreement
When I prayed to be delivered
Because of insincerity
My prayers were unheard.

Another day out of my head
I wasted so many years
The pain I felt from the loneliness
Caused so many tears.

I created a place
Which no one could enter
I didn't have to grow up
A fantasy world was rendered.

Back in nineteen eighty-four
God again knocked on my door
Sincerely I said, "Please, help me Lord,"
Now I have so much to be thankful for.

An addiction is beyond understanding
To the wise who have not entered in
Behind stonewalls they say
"Thank God I'm not like him."

They worship their exotic spirits
While abusing medical pills
Sitting on their judgment thrones
Unaware of their own ills.

Only a heart of love can truly see
Another's pain and agony
Free from your suffering you may be
If you truly want recovery.

I failed over and over again
But, I was given second chances
Before judging others
I consider my own circumstances. ©

Written by Gary Tucker 1-6-2011 ©

Acknowledgement, Desire, Recovery
Matt. 7:1-5, Luke 15:4-7, Luke 15:11-32

Journey Home Inspired by my aunt Beverly

Started out I wasn't feeling so well
Then the doctor had some news to tell
"You don't have much time, I'm so sorry"
I said to my friend "Let's have a party."

I want to see all my family, all my friends
Before my time here comes to an end
It may sound crude, but I've been blessed
From this frail body I'll have sweet rest.

Each painful day I'm drawn closer to my Lord
Some day this body will be restored
As my body grows weaker God's love seems stronger
I keep asking how much longer.

I'm looking forward to my journey home
It's good to know I won't travel alone
An angel from heaven will come for me
To take me where my Lord I'll see.

My new home is beyond the sky
I'll be there before you blink an eye
Gates of pearls and streets of gold
In my new home no one grows old.

I like to think I'll see you there
But, what Jesus said is very clear
"Unless you love Me and I dwell in your heart
"The glories of heaven you'll have no part."

There's no guarantee when it comes to living
Real life only comes when God is forgiving
Ask Jesus to save you and do it fast
This day, today may be your last.

Hope to see you on the other side
Where peace, love and joy abide
The choice is yours and yours alone
Follow me to a heavenly home.

I'm looking forward to my journey home
It's good to know I won't travel alone
With many others who've been atoned
Going to heaven where I'll never roam.

My heavenly home is beyond the sky
I'll be there before you blink an eye
Praising Jesus in all His glory
Forever thankful for the gospel story.

I'm looking forward to my journey home
It's good to know I won't travel alone
My heavenly home is beyond the sky
I'll be there before you blink an eye. ©

Written by Gary Tucker
9-2-2010

You'll Find Me
When You're Looking Down

When will you trust me, you know that I care
You're to blind to see your life's in despair
You want to live free but life isn't fair
I know your needs, more anguish you'll bear.

I love you more than all the sparrows
Walk in my path, its straight and narrow
Stay the course and there'll be no more sorrow
Not many more breaths you may borrow.

When life's too much for you to bear
Humble yourself and I'll be there
Abundant grace with you I'll share
Then you'll see how much I care.

When you think I'm nowhere to be found
You'll find me when you face the ground
Come to me where life abounds
You'll find me when you're looking down.

You say you're broke, I see what you're buying
To you life's a joke, soon you'll be crying
There's manna before you but you won't bend down
How much did you loose when you went up town?

It may be dull and yes it is dingy
Your heart says, "I need more than a penny"
You walk by it with a proud glance
I sent you some money; you took your stance.

When life's too much for you to bear
Humble yourself and I'll be there
Abundant grace with you I'll share
Then you'll see how much I care.

When you think I'm nowhere to be found
You'll find me when you face the ground
Come to me where life abounds
You'll find me when you're looking down.

I gave my life so you can live
A love for me you won't give
I feed you, cloth you, cover your head
When will you realize your soul is dead?

You love your life more than me
From your sins you must flee
Open you heart and you will see
Eternal life comes only from me.

When life's too much for you to bear
Humble yourself and I'll be there
Abundant grace with you I'll share.
Then you'll see how much I care.

When you think I'm nowhere to be found
You'll find me when you face the ground
Come to me where life abounds
You'll find me when you're looking down.
Humble yourself and I'll be there
You'll find me when you face the ground
Then you'll see how much I care
You'll find me when you're looking down. ©

Written by Gary Tucker © 9-2-2010

Army, Navy, Air Force, Marines

Written by Gary Tucker ©
8-6-2011

I'm proud to serve like my father before me
And fight with others to defend our country
No matter the challenge or trying condition
Beside my brothers it's a family tradition.

I may speak soft but carry big stick
When under attack I respond quick
To my enemy I say be forewarned
Marching to battle in my army uniform.

Sailing swiftly upon the high seas
More relentless than a nest of honey bees
When alarm bells ring feel her mighty sting
There's no escape from vengeance she flings.

Caves don't protect and if you ask why
No one hides from eagles in the sky
From many miles and x-ray vision eyes
When she drops her eggs be prepared to die.

The enemy can't hide under cover of night
Agile Marines have them in their sights
When they think they're safe and secure
Fierce judgment is speedily procured.

We know some won't return with the rest
They sacrificed their lives giving their best
Never forgotten though they be gone
With heart felt gratitude their memories live on.

As long as I have breath and strength to stand
I'll defend my country with gun in hand
With God as my friend I'll continue the fight
Defeating the enemy with holy might.

Weather Army, Navy, Air Force, Marines
No one stands against this fighting machine
Keeping the peace and protecting the week
I'm honored to defend what the oppressed seek. ©

Hills of Tennessee

I'm going home to the hills of Tennessee
I miss regal mountains where eagles soar free
When I can't walk and my eyes can't see
Carry me home to the hills of Tennessee.

There I'll lie still next to Father and Mother
Slumber in peace with Sister and Brother
I long to rest in the shadow of her hills
From valleys to peeks they are glory filled.

Her noble tips are crowned in royal smoke
As creeks flow gracefully down forest slopes
There's a place in my heart for Tennessee hills
When my final breath fades I'll love her still.

I'm going home to the hills of Tennessee
I miss regal mountains where eagles soar free
When I can't walk and my eyes can't see
Carry me home to the hills of Tennessee.

I'll take my last ride up that crooked dirt road
Over clear running streams to my new abode
The mountains await me for a long embrace
Until our creator returns with sweet grace.

Toward the east I'll see the morning star rise
Lighting the way for my Lord in the sky
Weep not for me 'cause I know what's in store
When my Master calls I'll rise alive evermore.

I'm going home to the hills of Tennessee
I miss regal mountains where eagles soar free
When I can't walk and my eyes can't see
Carry me home to the hills of Tennessee.

When I can't walk and my eyes can't see
Burry my bones in the hills of Tennessee. ©

Written by Gary Tucker
2-16-2011 ©

John the Baptist

Written by Gary Tucker 2-7-2011 ©
The birth of a prophet was foretold with explicit clues
Now is the time for this prophesy to come true
Within wombs of two women are Jesus and John
Two cousins born Spirit filled as time pressed on.

Elizabeth and Zacharias were old and with out child
They prayed to God and in time upon them He smiled
God opened her womb and there a son was conceived
With much love and joy baby John was received.

When he became of age he preached under the dessert sun
Baptizing believers and preparing the way for The Holy One
He wore a camel skin for clothing feeding on locust and honey
He had no house, mule, or land, not one coin for money.

He preached repentance of sins without flattery words
This angered Queen Herodias because of the truth she heard
She was unlawfully married to her king and begged to have him killed
The king refused but had him jailed until another prophesy fulfilled.

Herodias had a lovely daughter trained in seductive dance
Herod offered half his kingdom if he and his guest could have a glance
Mother and daughter conspired agreeing this was their chance
So she danced for the king until he yielded in hypnotic trance.

As agreed demanding of the king, "Upon your oath I now insist,
Deliver to me on a platter the head of John the Baptist."
The evil king was grieved, but granted her despicable request
He certainly couldn't renege on a promise witnessed by his guest.

That same night the ax fell and John's blood was spilled
The wicked queen eagerly waited to see the kings' order filled
She finally got what she longed for without even a fuss
John the Baptist is the greatest prophet there ever was. ©

I Believe I've Just Been Born Again

The preaching was strong
Powerful words not heard in so long
His message was contrary to the life I'd built
My soul felt heavy from the weight of guilt.

The sermon was over and he began to pray
"Heavenly Father, thank you for this glorious day
"Thank you for saving us in such a marvelous way
"Maybe there's someone here who's soul you'll save."

As I looked up I could see
The preacher was staring right at me
He said, "Let go of your sin
"And today you can be born again."

But, I held tight to the pew before me
I was afraid of what might be
"Do not delay and you can be free"
All the while he's looking at me.

The organ pipes were ringing
To the congregation's heart felt singing
"Just one more verse", I heard
"Then we'll have a closing word."

The organ pipes stopped ringing
As the congregation stopped singing
Then someone yelled out to say
"Wait for me I want to be saved today."

As I made my way up the isle
I was greeted by his smile
Said, "We've been praying for you Mr. Penn
"Are you ready to be born again?"

The organ pipes started ringing
To the congregation's heart felt singing
There were loud Hallelujahs and shouts of Amen
I believe, I believe, I've just been born again.

I believe, I believe, I've just been born again. ©

Written by Gary Tucker
10-30-2010

Old Time Religion

Written by Gary Tucker 12-14-2010

I'm going to an old time convention
To get some of that old time religion
The kind preached without detention
With intensions of a heavenly ascension.

Sitting in church pews week after week
Believing what every smooth talker speaks
Without opening the Bible to take a peek
They're deceived by wolves dressed as sheep.

Sitting in church pews month after month
The gospel of Christ preached not once
Holding souls ransom as she teaches subtle lies
Unaware of deception she's a devil in disguise.

Sitting in church pews year after year
Life saving Word withheld from their ears
Forsaking the truth they once held dear
Their eternal destiny is evidently clear.

So many churches have doused their light
There's no truth left in them to shine bright
To blind to see the condition of their plight
Their robes are spotted and no longer white.

So many churches across this land
With many names and different brands
They've become bacons of great wealth
At our expense through cleverness and stealth.

Why are churches lifeless and unspiritual?
It's because dead souls desire only a ritual
I'm going back to that old time religion
Because there's no hope in this new age rendition.

I'm going to an old time convention
To get some of that old time religion
The kind preached without detention
With intensions of a heavenly ascension. ©

Wish

Wish I had a voice to sing of God's abundant glory
I'd sing of His majesty and His redeeming story.

Wish I could write songs about God's graces
I'd write pages and pages to last through the ages.

Wish I could preach the gospel without reservation
I'd let the truth I speak convince people with persuasion.

Wish I had enough faith to walk upon water
I'd one step at a time walk closer to the Father.

Wish I had patience like Job when facing trials
I'd be more willing for my neighbor to walk an extra mile.

Wish I had a heart of love and compassion to offer
I'd reach out to others with help and words softer.

Wish I had courage like David facing the giant
I'd go out into the world showing the gospel to be reliant.

Wish I had strength like Samson fending off so many men
I'd be willing to fight righteous battles over and over again.

Wish I had wisdom like Salomon discerning right from wrong
I'd be able to make right decisions without taking so long.

Wish all these attributes I now attain
I'd be less inclined to whine and complain. ©

Written by Gary Tucker
11-21-2010 ©

What More Do I Need?

I have pillows on my bed
A roof over my head
I have a job that pays the bills
Suffer from no ills.

I'm so rich in this life
With friends and good wife
I have God's Word that feeds me
Why should I feel needy?

I don't need a fancy car
Or an airplane to fly me far
I don't need a lovely mansion
For worldly things I have no passion.

I don't need expensive clothes
At clearance sales I buy the most
I don't need a hefty bankroll
My soul might pay a heavy toll.

I don't worry about things to earthly
In a heavenly kingdom I'll live eternally
I don't lose sleep trying to count sheep
In blissful peace I always sleep.

I have angels watching over me
Some day their faces I'll see
I have God's love indeed
What more do I need? ©

Written by Gary Tucker
11-21-2010 ©

A Man From Galilee

(An Easter drama)

Choir
God loved us so much He sent His Holy Son
Whoever believes in Him will see a miracle done
His Spirit will renew us as lifeless souls become alive
Eternal death will loose its grip and Holiness will thrive.

The Immortal Son left Heaven to bare the sins of man
Retaining deity as man fulfilling Salvation's plan
Many words were written as the future was foretold
He walked among us thirty-three years as prophecies unfolded.

The Blessed Son has many names; perhaps you've heard of one
He is the great I AM, Savior, Christ and Holy One
He is Emanuel, Prince of Peace, a Mighty God to fear
Messiah, Counselor, King and others you'll soon hear.

Listen to this story for every word is true
He made a way to Heaven especially for you
Clear your mind and open your heart
Let today be the day you make a new start.

Narrator
There came a man from Galilee
Said He came to set men free
Born of a virgin without aid of earthly father
He came into this world to die upon an alter.

In Him is Life and a Light shining for all men
Because of darkness in men they could not comprehend
He is Alpha and Omega, the beginning and end
Broken relations with men He set out to mend.
Speaking in parables God's Word to proclaim

In Him men have hope; Jesus is His name
The poor became rich hearing Him preach
With wisdom and power He did teach.

He taught us how to live and go about our day
The purpose of life and how to God we should pray
We need not worry about things so earthly
He taught us what it meant to be spiritually worthy.

The lame He made walk and the blind to see
Others were possessed but Jesus set them free
The dead He made alive and limbs to grow
Bodies was deformed now look at them glow.

Diseases He healed and changed water into wine
Ears were unhearing but now they hear fine
He had a heart of love and spoke with God's authority
The people who loved Him were sadly the minority.

Performing miracles all the people to Him ran
But, the jealous Pharisees made an evil plan
They arrested Him and took Him by hand
Death to this Holy man was their demand.

Caiaphas asked Jesus, "Is it true what I heard?"
Before the high priest He said not a word
"I adjure You, Are You the Christ, the Son of God?"
"You have said it yourself," Jesus replied with a nod.

The high priest was so furious he tore his robe
They found their excuse; no need to further probe
"He's guilty of blasphemy; now He must die!"
This was their plan; they believed their own lie.

They took Him to Pilate, a governor of Rome
The deeds of a criminal he mustn't condone
They presented their lies and demanded he condemn
Pilate saw through them and found no fault in Him.

The governor spoke to have Jesus freed
But, the Pharisees wouldn't overcome their greed
Pilate offered the mob a trade in lieu
Barabbas, a killer or Jesus, King Of The Jews.

A fair offer the Jews did not perceive
How could they when they did not believe
The mob chose a killer to be set free
Pilate sent Jesus to die on a tree.

With a battered body and a crown of thorns
Marching to Golgotha to endure more scorn
It is written, "On behalf of the people one man must die"
Upon this lonely hill God's Lamb would be crucified.

Along with Jesus two other men hung
One mocking and one confessing with tongue
"Jesus, when You come into Your Kingdom, remember me"
Jesus replied, "With Me in Paradise Today you'll be."

Suffering on the cross this battle will soon be won
There's no other way for the Father's will to be done?
In agony He prayed to the Father that we be forgiven
While guards gambled for His garments to see what they'd be given.

Many gathered to watch the Lamb of God die
This was the Master's plan but no one understood why
The religious hypocrites were there mocking in fun
Saying, "Save Yourself if You truly are the Chosen One."

Then a cloud of darkness overtook the day
For the sins of the world a horrific price God will pay
"My God, My God, Why Have You Forsaken Me?"
"It Is Finished." With His final breath Jesus died to set men free.

As the demons were prowling the wind began howling
A loud crack spit the sky as angels could only stand by
How can man be justified by this One being crucified?
All heaven's host watched as He gave up the Ghost.

The earth was veiled in darkness to hide such pain and misery
Separation of Father from Son caused much anxiety
Jesus remained sinless to the very end
But the Father couldn't look upon Him because on Him lay my sin.

When Jesus said, "It is finished", Satan thought he'd won
He assumed the battle was finally over with the Blessed One
With temporary satisfaction he danced 'round Deaths' hill
Only an unholy mind could find such death a thrill.

Then the earth shook and rocks were split
From top to bottom the temple veil ripped
On Him God's wrath was poured without filter
The human cost was only thirty pieces of silver.

It was getting late so the Pharisees rushed things along
Complaining to Pilate, The criminals' deaths is taking to long
It's against our law for them to hang past three
Send guards to break legs of those hanging on trees.

Pilate sent word to guards on the hill
Proceed breaking legs at your discretion and will
They came to Jesus and found Him already dead
A guard pierced Him with a spear instead.

As was prophesized He had not a broken bone
From the cross to the tomb to be buried alone
The Pharisees asked Pilate to guard the tomb three days
So His disciples couldn't steal His body away.

After the Sabbath toward the fist day of the week
Came ladies named Mary; a look at the grave they seek
A severe earthquake occurred and an angle appeared
The guards became as dead and shook with great fear.

His appearance was like lightning with clothes white as snow
"What's happening here?" The women wanted to know
The angel rolled away the tombstone and then sat down
"He has risen, don't be afraid" to look around.

There were other tombs opened and saints were raised
Walking down city streets giving God all the praise
Now you would suppose this event would be much heard
So much happened in only thirty-four short words.

"Go tell His disciples He has risen from the dead
"He'll meet them in Galilee", not far up ahead
The sting of death men no longer need to fear
When they see Jesus It will all be made clear.

When Jesus met His disciples He explained His Father's will
"All things written of Me by the prophets must be fulfilled
"How I would suffer and rise from the dead the third day"
To die on a cross for mankind was the price I willingly paid.

He led them to Bethany after speaking these words
And blessing them He ascended from this world
With great joy the disciples worshipped Him
And continually praised God in song and hymns.

Disciple's song
He's alive, He has risen
Man can now be forgiven
He arose from the grave
Mankind can now be saved.

Glory to God, a new day has dawned
Praise to Jesus new life can spawn
When earthly bodies have expired
Judgment on the saved is not required.

The serpent thought he prevailed
When Jesus to the cross was nailed
What the devil didn't realize
From the grave He soon would rise.

As hard as demons tried
They could not prevent His rise
He's no longer on Death's side
Jesus Christ is glorified.

The Prince of Peace arose
He arose, He arose
The tomb could not contain Him
Shout it out, He arose.

Praise the Father, Praise the Son
Praise the Spirit, three in one
Praise the Father, Praise the Son
Praise the Spirit, Holy One.

Narrator
Twenty centuries have since passed and the story hasn't changed
The way to the Father through Jesus remains the same
If you repent from your sins and believe in His Holy name
You may dwell in Heaven without guilt or shame.

Our bodies are frail and grow so tired
We don't have much time before they expire
What we do in this life will decide our eternal fate
Ask Jesus to save you now before it's too late. ©

Written by Gary Tucker
2-7-2011

My Prayer

Written By Gary Tucker © 10-10-2010

Lord, please forgive me and hear my prayer
My broken heart is in need of repair
Extend your mercy and correct me from err
The guilt of my transgression is too much to bear.

You are the Almighty and one true God
You made all there is with less than a nod
You rule all creation with an outstretched rod
You watch over your children wherever they trod.

I've been the target of fierce fiery darts
Tempting me they've pierced my heart
From righteous ways I chose to part
To confess more sins, where shall I start?

The lust of my flesh I'm unable to tame
Day after day I sink deeper in shame
Disregarding Your Holy name
Parting myself from Your splendor and fame.

Lord, please forgive me and hear my prayer
My broken heart is in need of repair
Extend your mercy and correct me from err
The guilt of my transgression is too much to bear.

I use to walk close to you in Holy ways
Now I go my way and further I stray
I use to love You and do as You say
I use to look forward to a glorious day.

I want to do right, but I'm weak with no might
I long for peace, but its nowhere in sight
I've lost my way, alone in the night
Lord, I surrender I give up the fight.

Please restore me to the apple of Your eye
Guide me back home as you listen to me cry
Keep me safe in Your hand where Satan can't pry
Without your protection most surely I'd die.

Lord, please forgive me and hear my prayer
My broken heart is in need of repair
Extend your mercy and correct me from err
The guilt of my transgression is too much to bear.

Lord, you are omniscient, nothing's unknown
You are omnipotent, Strong Cornerstone
There's no hidden place unseen from Your throne
Thank you Lord, all my sins You atoned. ©

When The
Trumpet Sounds

When the trumpet sounds
Calling saints from the ground
Forsaking Death's shroud
To ascend through the clouds.

Far above earthly heights
To Heaven gleaming bright
Brighter than the stars
Its brilliance has no par.

Men's words can't describe
The grandeur viewed inside
Out of mortal's reach
Made with golden streets.

Standing face to face
With The King of Grace
Crowned with diadems
All knees bow to Him.

From His Holy Throne
Jesus calls His own
Giving us new names
No two are the same.

All tongues shall confess
All creatures shall profess
Resounding evermore
Jesus Christ is Lord.

When the trumpet sounds
Calling saints from the ground
Forsaking Death's shroud
To ascend through the clouds.

In harmonic voice
Saints sing and rejoice
Adoration loudly raise
As angels lend their praise.

Upon Golgotha's hill
Prophesies were fulfilled
Jesus was nailed to a cross
To redeem mankind lost.

He suffered there until
His death paid Ransom's bill
Taking my place to die
So I'd be made alive.

He redeems men that find
Release from sin that binds
With salvation freely given
Forgiving them their sins.

When cursed was my soul
God's love overflowed
Transforming a sinful heart
With holiness He imparts.

From two choices one make
When your soul is at stake
God offers life eternal
Sin offers death's infernal.

Won't you choose life?
And become a Holy wife
Partake of this mystery
As God's bride for eternity.

When the trumpet sounds
Calling saints from the ground
Forsaking Death's shroud
To ascend through the clouds.

In harmonic voice
Saints sing and rejoice
Adoration loudly raise
As angels lend their praise.
Jesus Christ is Lord
We adore Him evermore
To God be the glory
For what He did for me. ©

Written by Gary Tucker
7-15-2011

Starry Night

Starry night
Shining bright
Shedding light
Glorious sight.

Words of old
Had foretold
In the land
Of Bethlehem.

God's own son
The Chosen One
Came to men
His work defend.

Followed the star
From distance far
Came royal kings
Gifts to bring.

With much delight
Embraced the Light
Filled with joy
Seeing the Boy.

As then still now
The wise still bow
Presenting gifts
In morning mist.

Starry night
Shining bright
Shedding light
Glorious sight.

Starry night
Shining bright
Lighting the way
Men to save.

Words of old
Had foretold
Don't you know?
Blood must flow.

God's own son
Almighty One
On altar's cross
Suffered the cost.

Follow the star
From distance far
Escape prison bars
Where you are.

With much delight
Embrace the Light
Compelled to be
On bended knees.

As then still now
The wise still bow
Goodness persist
Gainst evil resist.

Starry night
Shining bright
Shedding light
Glorious sight.

Starry night
Shining bright
In our hearts
May it start.

Words of old
Had foretold
Breaking chains
Souls reclaimed.

God's own son
The Holy One
From sins be
Setting me free.

Followed the star
From distance far
Old life concedes
New life conceived.

With much delight
Embraced the light
I can rejoice
Triumphant voice.

As then still now
The wise still bow
Prayers I lift
As Spirit sifts.

Starry night
Shining bright
Shedding light
Glorious sight. ©

Written by Gary Tucker 8-2-2011 ©

New Jerusalem

Revelations 21, 22

With Heaven's gates open wide
Inviting saints to come inside
Hues of color not viewed by mortals
As we enter through pearly portals.

We'll walk on golden streets like glass
After walls of precious stones we pass
Made of jasper, sapphires and emeralds
New Jerusalem will radiate eternal.

As we're surrounded by Holy Light
Majestic creatures direct in flight
Pointing the way for all who enter
Guiding us toward smoke at the center.

As I come close I see a wondrous sight
From a throne shoots rays of light
A beautiful rainbow circles all 'round
As peals of thunder continually sound.

Upon the throne sits the Son of Man
With bronze feet should He choose to stand
His head and hair are white like snow
From His face comes the brightest glow.

I hear supreme power in His voice
Like the sound of many waters making noise
Anything tainted with sin and defies
Would be consumed by His fiery eyes.

Before Him I fall down as a lifeless man
In His presence I'm to scared to stand
Then to experience something so grand
Upon me God places His right hand.

"I'm the One who died and forever is alive
I'm Alfa and Omega, here you shall reside"
"Do not be afraid," I will hear Him say,
"I Am that I Am welcomes you here today".

Within His reach is the book of life
Containing names redeemed by the Light
All the saints will be given new names
And immortal bodies free of sin's chains.

From His throne flows water of life
Next to the river is the tree of life
Bearing twelve kinds of fruit to eat
Its healing leaves will nations reap.

There will no longer be any curse
Creation will be free of sinful lures
His words are faithful and they are true
God will again make all things new.

This is the day when saints rejoice
In unison sing with praiseful voice
Eternal life and happiness received
Reserved for those who in Jesus believed. ©

Written by Gary Tucker
9-15-2011

Be Strong in The Lord

Ephesians 6
Written by Gary Tucker 9-30-2011 ©

Prepare your feet to take a battle stand
With the gospel of peace firm in hand
Proclaim the Word throughout the land
For this is our Lord's command.

The gospel is a mysterious waste
To multitudes with lifeless souls
Pray for boldness to move with haste
So new life all mankind may know.

Be strong and courageous in the Lord
Advancing in His all powerful might
Be suited with God's protective armor
Prepare yourselves for a spiritual fight.

We struggle not with flesh and blood
But against rulers of a spiritual realm
Upon all creation their evil floods
With the great deceiver at their helm.

When the prince of darkness aims at you
Lift high your shield of faith
Stand firm girded in light and truth
Knowing only God's word can save.

Put on the helmet of salvation
To deflect deadly blows to your head
Use the Spirit's sword in anticipation
Against them that desire such dread.

Pray in the Spirit with un-blurred intuition
Laying before the alter humble supplications
Remain alert with perseverance and resolution
Working toward the day of our restoration.

Pray for ambassadors in willing chains
Preaching in confidence with His protection
Pray the Spirit guide you so you may attain
Life eternal magnifying His glorious perfection.

From our Creator the Father of love
And His blessed Son Jesus Christ
Peace be to saintly sisters and brothers
Grace rest upon you from Him on High. ©

Oh, Mighty God   A Sinner's Prayer

Oh, Mighty God I cry out to Thee
With a contrite heart hear my plea
Covered in shame and sinful stains
Naked and dirty bound by chains.

I come before You as a vessel of clay
Mold me and shape in Your perfect way
Only You know the sum of my days
Before barrowed time in this life fades.

I'm so thirsty and my soul is dry
Only drink from Your Fountain will satisfy
My body trembles with hunger panes
Only Your Bread of Life can sustain.

Forgive sinful deeds of my days past
Help me now perform works that last
Upon the alter I place selfish desires
As burdens are lifted like smoke from fire.

Look upon me now with merciful eyes
See a repentant man reaching toward the sky
Speak the words my ears long to hear
Say You forgive me in a way so clear.

Oh, Mighty God great are Your works
So many examples besides this earth
I ask You to perform a greater work in me
Make me Your servant counted as worthy.

I worship You and glorify Your name
From this day on I shall never be the same
You alone set me free with loving mercy
Renewing my life in preparation for eternity. ©

Friend,

Does Oh, Mighty God have any meaning for you? We are all born sinners bound by deathly chains. Some have been freed and received eternal life. Have you been released from chains that keep you separated from God? Only Merciful God can set us free. Does your soul feel dried up and lifeless? Do you hunger for something but find nothing fills you? Do you think you've committed so many sins that you can't be forgiven? The number of past sins makes no difference. Right now where you are make this your prayer in all sincerity. Ask God to forgive you for all sins past because only holy deeds will last. If this is your first sincere prayer then this is your first holy deed. May you now begin to glorify God with many good works, praises and thanksgivings as He prepares you for your journey to eternity.

Written by Gary Tucker © 10-1-2011

Valley of Fear

When you're in the valley of fear
And the road to peace is unclear
Life gives you more than you can bear
Call on a friend who is so dear.

When God's love seems so far away
No hope of getting through the day
Be still and listen to what I say
Bow your head and begin to pray.

When nothing seems to be going right
At the end of the tunnel you see no light
All you want is some rest tonight
Then pray to God with all your might.

When your life seems so pitiful poor
There's never enough and you need more
Pick yourself up off the floor
Just ask Jesus to open His store.

When you're in a fiery lake
And eternal life is at stake
The best decision you can make
Trust in Jesus your soul to take.

When you feel you're all alone
Among friends or even at home
When you're feeling tempted to roam
Trust in Jesus, the Cornerstone.

When you feel completely lost
From wave to wave you're being tossed
You want peace at any cost
Call on Jesus; He saves the lost.

When you feel you're on the hook
For something you haven't forsook
Read all about it in the Good Book
Turn the pages; it's worth a look.

When you feel life is unreal
What you do is no big deal
What you need is a spiritual meal
Feed on the Word; your soul it will heal.

When you feel you're under the gun
There's no place for you to run
In the shadows away from the sun
Turn to the Light, the Holy One. ©

Written by Gary Tucker
9-2-2010

I Pledge My Allegiance

Written by Gary Tucker 3-16-2011 ©

I stand at attention sincerely glad
As I pledge my allegiance to this flag
Symbolizing a republic for which she stands
Casting rays of independence over her land.

A fruited and bountiful land indivisible
Granting inalienable rights to individuals
Upon sovereign staff she waves free each day
Many mortals died to keep her this way.

A mighty nation under the guidance of God
His mercy protects her with a corrective rod
Constantly striving divine goals to reach
For instruction and virtues humbly beseech.

Outside her borders are heard amazing stories
Falling on captive ears yearning for her glories
Answering freedom's call to her they flee
Risking their lives crossing turbulent seas.

Declarations of liberty and justice resound
Free from oppression many have found
Finding equality and security within her stars
And peace received under red and white bars.

When Old Glory flies free and unfurled
Her colors reflect hope to an entire world
When asked what these colors acclaim
The United States of America proclaim.

When laws are righteous and judgment fair
Subjects live free and not in despair
When laws are corrupt and too heavy to bear
Peace and tranquility are viewed nowhere.

On bended knee I pray God's love for her endures
I will honor those who died keeping her pure
Upon my shoulders her burdens I'll gladly bear
May Stars and Stripes forever fly free raised high in the air. ©

I pledge allegiance to the flag
Of the United States of America
To the republic for which it stands
One nation under God, Indivisible
With liberty and justice for all.

Can you find the pledge in I Pledge My Allegiance?

America, How Sweet is Your Name

America, America, how sweet is your name
No other land equals your fame
Nations such as yours is all to few
There is no other that compares to you.

Home of eagles mighty and strong
Soaring though heaven in victor's song
Around the world with a heavy hand
Keeping peace with equitable demands.

Blessed with precious gems, silver and gold
More than King Solomon's temple could hold
To the world you open your food gates
Showing compassion from these United States.

From the Atlantic shores of Maine
To the Pacific islands of volcanic grains
Patrons gather for your anthem to sing
Listening to Liberty's bell in rhythm ring.

From southern beaches along Gulf of Mexico
To northern borders covered in snow
Many are called to share other's pain
And help their neighbor expecting no gain.

Thank you Lord, for those adorned in her uniform
And for a life sacrificed we truly mourn
I hope someday to shake their hand
In Heaven thank them for their courageous stand.

America's colors are red, white and blue
Honor and integrity waves beside truth
May her glorious symbol fly free and unfurled
Raised high upon her staff shining across the world. ©

Written by Gary Tucker
7-30-2011

Super Me

Who can leap tall buildings in a single bound?
Who can run faster than the speed of sound?
Who's stronger than a train and flies higher than a plane?
It's Super Me; let me explain.

Even though now I'm confined to this chair
With cloudy eyes and a heart needing repair
On the other side of death not far from here
I'll receive my new body and new clothes to wear.

I'll no longer need crutches to help me walk
I'll no longer need signs to help me talk
I'll no longer need glasses to help me see
An immortal body will be given to me.

Who can leap tall buildings in a single bound?
Who can run faster than the speed of sound?
Who's stronger than a train and flies higher than a plane?
It's Super Me; let me explain.

My new body will reflect God's glory
As laws of physics no longer control me
Without aid of transport I'll fly into space
And it's all because of God's wonderful grace.

I'll never grow old and I'll never die
No weapons to harm and no reasons why
All signs of warfare will disappear
We'll forever live in peace with no fear.

Who can leap tall buildings in a single bound?
Who can run faster than the speed of sound?
Who's stronger than a train and flies higher than a plane?
It's Super Me when I am changed. ©

Written by Gary Tucker 3-15-2011 ©

Poems
of Love

True Love Never Parts

Burning ambers start with sparks
Flaring in the depths of our hearts
Fanned by true loves' blowing
Constantly gleaming and glowing.

Beyond understanding but knowing
True love is always growing
Revealing tender feelings
True love is always showing.

Hearts are joined by one spark
That's how love always starts
Other emotions lose their devotions
But, true love never parts.

Crossing the barrier of time
True love developed refines
Tried and tested never reclines
True love matures sublime.

For true love many still seek
Peering into eyes of ones they meet
Searching their hearts for a spark
To see if true love can start.

Hearts are joined by one spark
That's how love always starts
Other emotions lose their devotions
But, true love never parts.

Written by Gary Tucker
5-21-2011 ©

My Little Boy Blue

They call him Blue, their five-year-old boy
He is their pride, their bundle of joy
With hair of gold and eyes so blue
Having fun in the park as they often do.

It was only a moment that dreadful day
Mom dropped her guard and Dad turned away
In a panic they ran to where he was playing
It was only a moment the swing was still swaying.

Mom started screaming as Dad yelled, too
Has anyone seen my little boy Blue?
With hair of gold and eyes so blue
Has anyone seen my little boy Blue?
With hair of gold and eyes so blue
Has anyone seen my little boy Blue?

The years took their toll and Mom fell ill
Finding Blue wasn't God's will
How long could she live with a heart so broke
After all the years she finally lost hope.

Dad made a promise before she died
Said he'd find Blue as he cried
His Blue was gone now his wife
How much more could he bear in this life?

Day after day the park Dad would visit
Passing the swing, he couldn't miss it
A dad and his boy were there to play
The dads shared a bench as it happened that day.

Surely they've met when they weren't as old
His eyes so blue and hair of gold
As dads were conversing young dad introduced
"Named after me this is my boy Blue."

Tears of joy filled Dad's eyes
He'd kept his promise then looked to the sky
Said, "Thank you Lord and please tell my wife
"I finally found him, the joy of our lives."

My dad was shouting with a joyful sound
"He once was lost but now he's found
This is my boy, my little boy Blue
I finally found my little boy Blue."
"He once was lost but now he's found
I finally found my little boy Blue." ©

Written by Gary Tucker
9-2-2010

I'm so Sorry

Written by Gary Tucker ©
8-9-2011

Can't recall when we last loved
Seems we both have given up
Happiness shared was short lived
This selfish man, can you forgive?

I don't see smiles you use to wear
Your eyes are often filled with tears
We don't share dreams like before
You don't say you love me anymore.

I'm so sorry I caused you pain
I'm so sorry you feel ashamed
How could I have been so cruel?
Disregarding marriage rules.

Your silence cries out for help
Arms don't reach out to be held
Avoiding the need to be kissed
Past closeness is sorely missed.

Vainly thinking only of myself
Like a book put you on a shelf
You stood by me remaining true
To blind to see love for me in you.

Can you forgive this selfish man?
Can you love me as I am?
I promise to change my ways
And give you all my remaining days.

I'm so sorry I caused you pain
I'm so sorry you feel ashamed
How could I have been so cruel?
Disregarding marriage rules.

Can you forgive this selfish man?
Can you love me as I am?
I promise to change my ways
And give you all my remaining days. ©

My One And Only
True Love

I never thought I could feel this way
You're on my mind all through the day
We fit together like a hand in glove
You are my one and only true love.

For you I wished upon a star
Now we're here in each other's arms
Until the end of time you'll always be
My one and only true love.

You're my night in shining armor
You're what my heart was pining for
A damsel waiting patiently
For my champion to reveal himself to me.

With true love to impart
You filled my empty heart
More and more bestowing
Beyond the point of overflowing.

The light in your eyes
Reflect love like a grand sunrise
Shining rays of color bright
A magnificent glorious sight.

The smiles you give to me
Are precious abundantly
Loving words you speak with ease
My ears hear them frequently.

Your touch is soft and gentle
Your kisses are plentiful
You treat me like a princess
With thoughtfulness and kindness.

You bring me pretty flowers
With lovely gifts you often shower
But, your love for this girl
I value more than priceless pearls.

I never thought I could feel this way
You're on my mind all through the day
We fit together like a hand in glove
You are my one and only true love.

For you I wished upon a star
Now we're here in each other's arms
Until the end of time you'll always be
My one and only true love. ©

Written by Gary Tucker
5-19-2011 ©

Little John

I heard a knock on the door
A man dressed in uniform
Said, "Your beloved had fallen
He was sorry to inform."

"He was so brave
Because of him I'm alive
Five men he saved
I'm one of the lucky five."

As I broke down in tears
He asked, "Is there family you can call?"
He tried to relieve my fears
My husband and I, that is all.

I knew this day might come
But, I was praying not today
Today's our anniversary
And there's a baby on the way.

As he spoke words of comfort
I saw tears form in his eyes
He began to tremble
And we both cried.

"Your husband and I were friends
He spoke with love of his Emily
Wish it were me instead of him
I have no family."

And that's how it began
Two weary souls
Became a new family
Not so long ago.

Together we raise Little John
He's proud to be his father's son.
In him his dad lives on
Reminding us of our fallen one. ©

Written by Gary Tucker
10-11-2010

Happy Daze Written by Gary Tucker © 4-12-2011

I have this thing called love sickness
So I run to my doctor for his analysis
He says, "I can treat you in only one way
Are you prepared to experience happy daze?"

"My treatment doesn't require any pills
Taking care of you requires hands on skills
I'm honored and consider it a thrill
When you come back to me for all your refills."

I make appointments so we can be alone
Because I can't wait for him to get home
In the examination room just as I planned
This is one place where the doctor gets exam-ed.

I don't need a stethoscope to hear his heart race
We don't have much time so we move with haste
Four appointment times pass so I really should go
But, it's hard for us to part when our hearts say no.

Leaving the office nurses see my happy daze
Wishing their husbands could satisfy their crave
I say, "Keep his schedule open each and every day
Tomorrow looks like another happy daze."

When we're together romance gets outrageous
Because my love sickness is so contagious
I'm his number one patient without having to pay
He's my patient too, and enjoys his happy daze.

Playing doctor isn't just for young friends
I married me one so the playing never ends
With him each day shines glorious sunrays
The forecast looks bright for many happy daze. ©

Mishym, My Genie

I was exploring a forgotten desert land
When I spotted a shimmer in the sand
I knelt down to see what I'd found
It's just an old oil lamp on the ground.

I was intrigued so I took it back to camp
There I saw six letters inscribed on the lamp
It was dirty so I began to wipe it clean
You had to be there to believe what I'd seen.

The lamp began to smoke and shake
Before my eyes a lovely female took shape
Was this a dream or was I awake?
She took her pose and I started to quake.

I couldn't speak for her beauty over whelmed me
I couldn't move for Cupid's arrow nailed me
I couldn't look away for her eyes stared upon me
I couldn't believe this was happening to me.

My name is Mishym and I'm old as the sands of time
I've troubled many kings with this simple rhyme
Where academics have failed perhaps you'll succeed
Do one thing for me and I'll fulfill your deepest need.

I'll grant your wish if on time you answer this riddle
What shakes mountains with just subtle ripple?
What makes the earth tremor with a magnitude of eight?
Hurry; the sands in my hourglass will tell if you're late.

(Can you solve the riddle without reading further?)

I thought about Mishym and her rhyme
Could I find the answer in an hour's time?
If I answer her riddle which no one's been privy
She'll grant my desire only a Genie can give me.

After careful thought I considered her name
It must have some forgotten ancient fame
Rearrange the letters and what do I see?
An enchantress with the power of Shimmy.

You are the glass that holds dust of the earth
You make mountains erupt with great burst
You are the ground that violently sways
Shimmy is the answer to your mystery I say?

Many rulers over many empires have failed
To give the correct answer but you prevailed
I'm at your command to do as you require
Reveal to me your heart's desire.

I have no desire for gold or such wealth
I need a woman beside me in sickness or health
My life is empty and love is past due
To feel the touch of someone lovely like you.

I desire someone to share my life
Would it be too much to ask if you'd be my wife?
I did my best answering your rhyme
Will you stay with me for the rest of my time? ©

Written by Gary Tucker
12-21-2010

Shimmy Wife

With rings on her fingers
And tassels on her clothes
Her titillating scent lingers
She's quite a voluptuous host.

Tonight she's my expedition guide
Leading me places I'll not forget
She's taking me on a pleasure ride
Guaranteed with no regrets.

Her beckoning arms begin to slither
As mountains start to shake
Down below the earth quakes
With tremors of magnitude eight.

To every note and every chord
She glides in rhythm about the floor
Side to side hips snap and roll
Inner sensations I control no more.

Like a piston on a locomotive
Working up to speed
Every motion tells a story
If you know how to read.

She camel shimmies all round me
She's got me hypnotized
With such ease she lifts and pops
Now I'm mesmerized.

She gives her heart away
Back again she takes it
With her flame I'm set on fire
No amount of rain can douse it.

Each quiver excites my body
As I watch her swoop and sway.
Each ripple ignites my spirit
My eyes can't look away.

Her peacock takes flight
All her vibrations are in tune
I'm the luckiest man alive
It's at me she directs her woo.

She cast her enchanting spell
With passion I'm now inflamed
I find her magic irresistible
This desire can't be tamed.

This pleasure guide is my shimmy wife
She shimmies just for me
Dancing for my pleasure
Because I'm her one and only.

Tomorrow I'll cast my charms
So her desires can be set free
I'll dance for her pleasure
Because she's my one and only. ©

Written by Gary Tucker
12-12-2010

(Husbands and wives, take your
romance to a higher level with Shimmy.)

Wedding Night Heart Failure

Written by Gary Tucker 8-31-2010

Walking down the isle with flowers in your hair
With grace and style you are most fair
You gave me your hand; I gave you my life
Before all we stand, I make you my wife.

After the pictures we drove to the hall
Like a fairy tail dream we're off to the ball
The food was catered; we spared no expense
Not much later we started to dance.

Glasses were raised and good wishes made
Shared words of praise as the night quickly fades
Thanks everyone but, we must now part
To where another aspect of our love may start.

The room was aglow from the moon above
As we prepared for a night of love
The look in her eye; come get me lure
In each other's arms we'll know love's pleasures.

My heart was pounding; my blood was flowing
Unfamiliar sensations and still not knowing
Life can sometimes be unsure
How was I to know I was having heart failure?

The medics came but not in time
To the room where I was cut down in my prime
Now I must leave you my dear wife
Without ever knowing what your love is like.

Guess I'll never know a pure love united
Perhaps in the after life we'll be reunited
We did our best keeping our love pure
Life's not guaranteed, that's for sure. ©

Tongue—Tied and Sh, Sh, Shy

For Him

I met the woman of my dreams
I can't tell her what this means
Because when she says "Hi"
I get tongue-tied and sh-sh-shy.

She has long wavy hair
We'll make a handsome pair
But, when she looks me in the eye
I freeze up and want to die.

She has a voice soft and gentle
She has the cutest dimples
When she says good-by
I just want to cry.

How can I tell her she's for me?
How can I tell her so she'll see?
I'm not just another guy
Telling flirty lies.

I love her from head to toes
Does she know? Don't say no
Cupid's arrow pierced my heart
It's aglow. Does it show?

She probably thinks I'm a geek
Tripping over my own two feet
My will is strong, but courage week
I can't find the words to speak.

What can I do when words are few?
When I'm with her, my lips feel glued
How can I relay when it's just we two?
What can I say except I love you. ©

Written by Gary Tucker 1-3-2011 ©

Tongue—Tied and Sh, Sh, Shy

For Her

I met the man of my dreams
I can't tell him what this means
Because when he says "Hi"
I get tongue-tied and sh-sh-shy.

His eyes sparkle and glare
We'll make a lovely pair
But, when he looks me in the eye
I panic and want to fly.

His voice is strong and soothing
With him I'd like some smooching
And when he walks by
I can't control my sigh.

How can I tell him he's for me?
How can I tell him so he'll see?
I'm not trying to be sly
Telling romantic lies.

I love him and his button nose
Does he know? Don't say no
Cupid's arrow pierced my heart
Rapture flows. Does it show?

I'd love to be his princess
Dance with him in a fancy dress
But, I'm under much duress
My words come out in such a mess.

How can I relay I think he's cute?
When I'm with him, my lips feel mute
What can I do when words are few?
All I can say is I love you. ©

Savant (A)

Written by Gary Tucker 3-16-2011 ©

My wife is a savant
She knows what I want
Her love is made clear
She's a modern day seer.

When her day weighs a heavy toll
She runs to me to be consoled
When I wrap her in my arms
She's relieved and unalarmed.

And then she looks up at me
With eyes bluer than the sky
And she loves me
Like no other could love me.

Because she's a savant
She knows what I want
Her love is made clear
She's a modern day seer.

Her love is so pure
I'm addicted for sure
I can't live without her
How would I endure?

The sparks in her kiss
Are all for me she insist
When she nibbles on my ear
There's no resistance near.

Then she holds me tight
And loves me with all her might
Her passion is uncanny
As love sometimes can be.

Because she's a savant
She knows what I want
Her love is made clear
She's a modern day seer.

The glide in her walk
Her gentle talk
Her soft touch
Oh, I love her so much.

Because she's a savant
She knows what I want
Her love is made clear
She's a modern day seer. ©

Savant (B)

My wife says I'm a savant
Because I know what she wants
My love is made clear
I'm a modern day seer.

I can't fix a car
Or carry a conversation far
I stand firm by her side
I'm her anchor in life's tide.

When her day weights a heavy toll
She runs to me to be consoled
We hold tight in each other's arms
Where she no longer feels alarmed.

And then she looks up at me
With eyes bluer than the sky
And I love her
Like no other man can love her.

Because I'm a savant
I know what she wants
My love is made clear
I'm a modern day seer.

My love is a drug not in bought in stores
I give it all to one I adore
She can't live with out it
There's no doubt about it.

I see it in her face
I feel it in her embrace
I see it in her eyes
I feel it in her sighs.

My love she can't resist
I feel it in her kiss
She opens up her heart
Where true love I do impart.

Because I'm a savant
I know what she wants
My love is made clear
I'm a modern day seer.

I know when she wants me
And how love needs to be
I give her space to be free
But, in hast she returns to me.

Because I'm a savant
I know what she wants
My love is made clear
I'm a modern day seer. ©

Written by Gary Tucker
3-16-2011

Tippin' the Bottle

Sittin' in my chair
I ain't goin' nowhere
I got nothin' to do
Just reminiscing of you.

Questions fill my head
Was it something I said?
What did I do wrong?
You been gone for so long.

Memories of us two
I was so in love with you
Why'd you leave me here alone?
Will you ever come back home?

Swore I'd never do it
But, no one's here to prove it
Full speed at full throttle
You got me tippin' the bottle.

Why'd you have to leave me, Darlin'?
Why'd you have to grieve me, Darlin'?
Why must you deceive me, Darlin'?
Why must you be free of me, my Darlin'?

I finally got the call of dread
Telling me you were dead
Victim of a hit and run
What on Earth has someone done?

You were once my best friend
You were there thru thick and thin
You brought comfort to my heart
Rays of sunlight on days dark.

I took you in as a stray
Roaming eyes wouldn't let you stay
Like a bullet shot from a gun
You saw your chance and made a run.

I begged and pleaded to no avail
But you ran off with some other male
Friends say I'll find someone new
But my heart's still stuck on you.

You broke my heart leaving me alone
No one to greet me when I come home
Your loving kisses I'll surly miss
Having you back is what I wish.

You ran away like a dog in heat
For your devotion I can't compete
Romping with tramps near and far
There's a word for what you are.

Swore I'd never do it
But, no one's here to prove it
Full speed at full throttle
You got me tippin' the bottle.

Why'd you have to leave me, Darlin'?
Why'd you have to grieve me, Darlin'?
Why must you deceive me, Darlin'?
Why must you be free of me, my Darlin'? ©

Written by Gary Tucker © 8-24-2011

(You don't think I'd start tipping the bottle over a woman
do you? I provided clues, one obvious, as to whom Darlin' is.)

Only In My Dreams

Got a call at work from the wife
Said, "Hurry home if you want some excitement in your life"
I rushed home to see what she had in store
An opened door revealed rose petals on the floor.

L'mour's perfume was abundant in the air
Its captivating scent led me up the bedroom stairs
There I viewed my wife dressed only in a thong
Moving and grooving to our favorite love song.

My elation was overwhelming, not felt in many years
She beckoned me closer and whispered in my ear
Said, "Prepare yourself for some excitement in you life
I'm going to make you glad you chose me for a wife."

She ripped the clothes off my body and began to sway
"Oh Lord," I prayed, "Give me stamina to last through this day."
She held me close and tight while kissing on my ear
The next thing on her mind was made perfectly clear.

She laid me down and she . . . and she . . . and she . . .
BEEP! BEEP! BEEP! BEEP! BEEP! BEEP!

"What's that noise?" It sounds familiar
Please let nothing interrupt romantic pleasure
I opened my eyes and then understood
The alarm clock was robbing me of my manly-hood.

I turned it off and tried again to sleep
But the wife in my dream I was unable to keep
In desperation I rolled over to my wife
Saying, "You want some excitement in your life?"

She mumbled the words, "Only in your dreams"
Seems excitement in my life is an illusion unredeemed
So tomorrow night I'll close my eyes and love her only in my dreams
Tomorrow night I'll unplug the clock and love her only in my dreams. ©

Written by Gary Tucker © 4-13-2011

Lover's Dream

When the day turns to night and I'm alone
I close my eyes and dream of my romantic place
There my beloved waits with ever reaching arms
Ready to be enveloped in a lover's embrace.

His voice is strong but soothing
It ignites the woman inside me
Like sparks in a roaring fire
Flames of passion burn profusely.

I inhale the scent of his body
And like the perfume of a rose
It's enticing and warm
Drawing me closer and closer.

His eyes sparkle like stars
In the darkest of the night
I get quivers deep within
As I'm touched with delight.

As eager lips come together
I feel my lover's faint tremor
He whispers words of adulation
While love pours out like a river.

Like a tropical monsoon
His love fuels my yearning heart
My lover's so real to me
I feel each beat of his heart.

The sun will soon be rising
And I must take my leave
We'll be together soon
If I only believe.

We'll be apart for a while
A life time though it seems
Tomorrow night I'll close my eyes
And love you only in my dreams.

Tomorrow night I'll close my eyes
And love you only in my dreams. ©

Written by Gary Tucker
10-10-2010

Poems for Life's Lessons

Messed Up Life

Over thirty years of a messed up life
Worse and worse becomes the strife
For a bad decision I pay a high price
All because I chose the wrong wife.

Before you rush to a lifetime of grief
And suffer for years with no relief
Don't let stupid rob you like a thief
A wrong wife bites with sharp teeth.

I know you think she's the one
And you're having loads of fun
This lovely sexpot you have won
Take my advice young man and run.

Her lure and beauty will soon fade
For another wife you'll wish to trade
Marriage is more than getting laid
And that quickly gets a failing grade.

If you have any good sense at all
Think with your big head not the small
Be wise and avoid many squalls
Or be like a steer with tied off

 ©

Written by Gary Tucker
11-13-2010

Some Don't Know

Some don't know the hell of battlegrounds
Where death and misery abounds all around
Some don't know the torture in my mind
When having to leave best friend behind.

Some don't know the heavy sorrow I bear
Never goers away, it's too painful to share
To find I harmed comrades in friendly fire
Do I end it now or escape from this mire?

Some don't know the angry words I hear
Departing the plane to screaming jeers
To be the object of ridicule robust
The placards say, "God hates your guts".

Some don't know and have no desire to learn
From right and wrong they can't discern
Some don't know evil must be fought
To love one's country they haven't been taught.

Some don't know for lack of knowledge
Protesting secured in their local college
While being bombarded with endless rounds
Our transport's been hit and we're going down.

Some don't know the meaning of honor
To stand upright they won't even ponder
Some don't know or care for their neighbor
Contempt and disgust in their hearts harbor.

Some don't know the conflicts raging inside
With each battle new monsters within hide
While I keep my demons under control
Some let theirs lose to wage a heavy toll.

Some don't know with missing leg or arm
How my scarred body causes stare and alarm
I returned home with a body sorely battered
Others returned with minds completely shattered.

Some don't know how to fight a war
They sit in an office demanding we give more
They make up silly rules and take away our guns
If it were up to them our wars would not be won.

Some don't know because to them it's unreal
When distant troubles are all but concealed
Waving white flag with surrender they find
While liberty and freedom is always on my mind.

Some don't know the horrific sounds of death
I will remember them till my final breath
Some don't know because they muted the sound
In the back of my head they forever resound.

Some don't know and they never will
Their cup of happiness will never be filled
I'm an American soldier in case you don't know
Humbled, as heartfelt gratitude overflows
from most. ©

Written by Gary Tucker
8-7-2011

America, America,
Why Can't You See?

America, America, why can't you see
You once were a nation mighty and free
It wasn't long ago; remember when?
But, now your stars are glowing dim.

Your leaders have become corrupt and shallow
Their flattery words are empty and hollow
No one listens or respects them anymore
They've been caught stealing from your money stores.

In darkness sinners conspire to snuff out your life
By inciting your people with envy and strife
Your enemies dwell freely within your borders
Receiving commands with decisive orders.

You once stood for liberty and justice for all
Now your judges create their own laws
Detesting what the constitution declares
Arrogantly deeming it outdated and unfair.

By millions your littlest ones are dying
Disregarding precious life inside crying
Quietly it's all done out of sight
Because mothers are told it's their right.

Wake up Lady Liberty and open your eyes
Some among you spread deception and lies
Can't you see they plot your falling?
Remember your summons with holy calling.

God raised you up to shine across tidal seas
But, you scuttled your ship with no lifeguard to save thee
In much distress you're about to drown
Your once glorious symbol now flies upside down.

America, America, why can't you see?
A working lighthouse again you may be
Consider selecting servants in righteousness walking
Or sink electing criminals with the gift of double-talking. ©

Written by Gary Tucker
3-23-2011

"Ask not what America will do for you,
But rather what together we can do for the freedom of men."
USA President, John F. Kennedy

Jailhouse Baby

I was blinded by his charm
Felt good wrapped in his arms
Overlooked his brutish flaws
Even the bruises on my jaw.

We had good times in the night
I was a fool to think that's right
I must be insane
Here each day to awake in pain.

When he found I was with child
He got so violent and riled
I knew I had to leave
But, for me there's no reprieve.

The law couldn't help me
Their legal minds wouldn't listen
I was left with one decision
They all seemed to be missin'.
I'll do what I must do
So we both can survive
I'll do what I must do
So you'll be born alive.

One night it got real rough
I'd finally had enough
This lesson I'll surely teach
As for his gun I reached

Lay a hand on me again
And this will be your end
I saw great anger in his stare
A piercing evil glare.

Like a bull he came charging
His rage was enlarging
Gun smokes' in the air
No more abuse I'll have to bear.

The law couldn't help me
Their legal minds wouldn't listen
I was left with one decision
They all seemed to be missin'.
I'll do what I must do

So we both can survive
I'll do what I must do
So you'll be born alive.

On the floor he lay
For his cruelty he'll now pay
Could it be that we're now free
No more harm for baby and me.

Before I even took the stand
The D.A. shook the judge's hand
"I'll thank you for a speedy trial"
"Already have the sentence filed."

As I stood before my peers
There were many jeers
I explained how he'd mistreat me
But they chose not to believe me.

The law couldn't help me
Their legal minds wouldn't listen
I was left with one decision
They all seemed to be missin'.
I did what I did
So we both would survive
I did what I did
So you'd be born alive.

Some say I did you daddy wrong
And I'm right where I belong
But, they weren't there to see
All the agony he gave to me.

I thank my lucky stars
For protecting you so far
Ironically we're safer here
Behind these iron bars.

Do I have regrets?
I have one for you young lady
Honey, I'm so sorry
You were born a jailhouse baby.

The law couldn't help me
Their legal minds wouldn't listen
I was left with one decision
They all seemed to be missin'.
I did what I did
So we both would survive
I did what I did
So you'd be born alive.

I'm so sorry young lady
You were born a jailhouse baby
I want you to know I'll always love you
I'll always love you, my jailhouse baby. ©

Written by Gary Tucker
10-11-2010

What Do You See?

What do you see
When you look into a mirror?
First clean the glass
So you can see clear.

Look past your face
Deep into your eyes
Ignore your surroundings
They only lie.

Down to your heart
So you can see the true you
Only there can you start
To see what you value.

Do you see envy?
Always wanting
Maybe there's pride
Always taunting.

For your neighbor
Does it care?
Will it raise
Him up in prayer?

Most importantly
Is it filled with love?
Does it have peace
With God above?

When you look at me
Do you see a potential friend?
Or are you unable to see past
The color of my skin?

Look past my face
Deep into my eyes
Ignore my surroundings
They only lie.

When you look into the mirror
What do you see?
Seeing a little clearer
Someone who's still better than me? ©

Written by Gary Tucker
10-23-2010

Married and Clueless

A duet poem, Husband first, Wife second and both together

We were young and running wild,
    You were my heartbeat's poster child.
We were active all the time,
    Playing and traveling in our prime.
You begged me to live with you,
    You asked me to be true.
Before I knew it I was married and clueless,
    Sometimes a girl has to be ruthless.
Your favorite words became "Don't touch!'
    I think you've had enough.
The kids are now grown and out the door,
    Just the two of us penniless and poor.
Now we don't play nor do we travel,
    I bet on you and lost the gamble.
This should be the best time of our lives,
    You no longer make me feel alive.
From separate beds to separate rooms,
    Maybe I should find a younger groom.

What happened to us, I thought we were in love
You were the one I was always thinking of
We had so much fun before we were married
But, now being with you makes me feel so wary.

Remember the time we drove to Reno?
    We had so much fun in that El Camino
Remember the time we sailed the Bahamas?
    And flew to Tibet to see the Dalai Lama.

What happened to us, I thought we were in love
You were the one I was always thinking of
We had so much fun before we were married
But, now being with you makes me feel so wary.

You really let yourself go, Floe,
　That's not what your brother says, Joe.
You don't comb your hair,
　You don't buy me new clothes to wear.
You stay out all night,
　You're making me uptight.
You are so lazy,
　You're driving me crazy.
You don't clean the house,
　You're such a louse.
You put a scratch on my car,
　I'll put a penny in your jar.
You have smelly feet,
　You don't put down the seat.
You were once a heartthrob,
　Why don't you get a job?
After forty-two years I'm still clueless,
　It's been thirty-two years and you're still useless.

What happened to us, I thought we were in love
You were the one I was always thinking of
We had so much fun before we were married
But, now being with you makes me feel so wary. ©

Written by Gary Tucker
10-27-2010

Virtues

Written by Gary Tucker
10-31-2010

So you think you're in love
He's like an angel from above
He sends you pretty flowers
With lovely gifts he does shower.

You each have pet names
He offers attention and fame
You just lost one boy friend
Can't let that happen again.

He says you're a wondrous sight
Dressed in revealing clothes skintight
He looks you over up and down
Checking you out from all around.

His hands are all over you
And you still haven't a clue
The boy wants more than a kiss
And he knows you won't resist.

You trusted your heart but it lied
He takes it all in stride
The purity you had you now lack
And you can never get it back.

Before unlearned virtues come to late
Keep yourself pure when looking for a mate
Seek a virtuous man who desires to be holy
Flee from all others; seek godly ones only.

In regards to your attire
This virtue he should admire
Long, loose and lots
Don't show off what you've got.

In regards to your temple
This virtue is so simple
Knowledge and purity is wealth
Keep your hands and lips to your self.

In regards to your speech
Every pastor should preach
A virtue that shouldn't be buried
Don't speak as if you're married. ©

POW! POW! POW!

POW! POW! POW!
I heard ringing in the night
POW! POW! POW!
More gunshots; what a fright.

Two bodies lying in the street
Off to their maker tonight they'll meet
Why did these two have to die?
Can anyone tell me why?

As families gathered hugging
They pondered this awful mugging
Did they die because of drugs?
Who were the violent thugs?

It's not safe on city streets
Be wary of strangers that you meet
Don't be fooled by their friendly smile
Under that facade lies murder and vile.

Today peoples' lives have no value
For a buck some would even kill you
Before the night's over more will die
And more families will be asking why?

POW! POW! POW!
I heard ringing in the night
POW! POW! POW!
More gunshots; what a fright. ©

Written by Gary Tucker
11-27-2010

Happy Ever After

After years of paying my dues
What do I get for loving you?
Many years of heartache and blues
That's what I get for loving you.

You're out night after night
All the unknowns give me a fright
It's late and you're nowhere in sight
There'll be no loving you tonight.

In the morning you finally come home
No explanation, you could at least phone
Nighttime awaits and you'll be off to roam
Leaving me here all alone.

I'm so tired of all this rejection
My life needs a serious correction
No more time for love's deflection
I'm setting course for a new direction.

I don't know what lies ahead
But, years of anxiety I'll soon shed
In a fairy tale book I once read
A new life awaits me, so it said.

My destiny I'm ready to master
I'm moving forward faster and faster
I'm going to find my 'happy ever after'
It's a life full of love and laughter. ©

Written by Gary Tucker
11-13-2010

Can You Hear Me?

I hear voices but they're blurred, I think they're asking why?
So many questions but I'm unable to reply.
What's your name? How many fingers do you see?
How many did you take? Can you even hear me?

This must be a dream; I'm confused and dazed
My head is spinning in so many ways.
Needles in my arm, a tube in my mouth
Strapped down, can't move, someone's cutting off my blouse.

"Why'd you do it?" the doctor asked. "We lose patients every day
They would love a new lease on life; yours nearly slipped away."
Every year at Christmas time we fill our lives with stuff
Everyone expects too much, they can't seem to get enough.

People spend their lives in debt and they do it with such cheer
I'm about to lose my house; I can't afford gifts one more year.
Even though my cupboard's bare still everyone wants more
Does anyone remember what is this season's truly for? ©

Gifts This Year?

What do think will happen if you celebrate without gifts this year?
Your family, friends and coworkers will no longer hold you dear.
So don't say "Jesus is the reason for the season"
When our carnal lives demand gifts by legions. ©

Written by Gary Tucker 12-14-2010

I'm Through With You

Put down in front of your friends
Your criticism never ends
At parties I'm left standing alone
I'd have more fun if I stayed home.

Your lips are cold like ice
Your demeanor's less than nice
If this is the best you can do
Baby, Baby, I'm through with you.

I know your heart's been cheatin'
With other girls you been mistreatin'
Their strong scent's all over you
Baby, Baby, I'm through with you.

I'm through with your roaming eyes
I'm through with your many lies
I'm through with you makin' me blue
Baby, Baby, I'm through with you.

At the party I saw you and Sue
In each other's arms were you two
If you think I haven't a clue
Baby, Baby, I'm on to you.

A little later you both disappeared
And reappeared with lipstick on your ear
Hear something long over due
Baby, Baby, I'm through with you.

How could I have been so naive?
With open eyes I now can see
No more will I be deceived
Baby, Baby, I'm setting me free.

My lovin's too good for you
I'm going to find me somebody new
Hear one thing absolutely true
Baby, Baby, I'm through with you.

In case you still haven't heard
I'm through with your hurtin' words
Don't turn away from my point of view
Baby, Baby, I'm through with you. ©

Written by Gary Tucker
5-17-2011

Down Sizin'

With new friends you're out drinkin'
You stay in bed all day slinkin'
At other guys you've been winkin'
Girl, what could you be thinkin'?

When I try to kiss you turn away
When I try to hold you move away
Words of love you won't say
You're so close but far away.

You built walls keeping us apart
Your neglect cuts to my heart
It's to late for a new start
I think it's time for us to part.

I won't hear you say,
"Don't touch me," anymore
You won't hear me say
"I love you," anymore.

Just one last thing to say
I can't take this anymore
Before the mornin' sun's risin'
I'll be down sizin'.

You won't feel me touch you anymore
Cause I won't reach for you no more
I won't trouble you for a kiss
I'll find someone else with ruby lips.

I won't hear you say,
"Don't touch me," anymore
And you won't hear me say
"I love you," anymore.

Just one last thing to say
I can't take this anymore
Before the mornin' sun's risin'
I'll be down sizin'. ©

Written by Gary Tucker
7-27-2011

About the author

I didn't particularly like to read as a kid. I especially didn't like poetry. Traditional poetry was to difficult to understand and from what I see on the internet that hasn't changed for me. After retiring I decided to write down some ideas from years past in a way that's easy for everyone young and old to understand. After all, what's the use of writing if the reader can't understand what's attempted to be expressed?

You can find a smaller version of my poems suitable for church in **Oh Lord, Tell Me Why,** which includes all my inspirational poems plus a few others.

It would be my pleasure to share with you some laughs, hopes, dreams and lessons learned over the years. Please let me know if I have succeeded at gltgassy@aim.com.

May God bless you,
Gary L. Tucker